ANTIFA

The Complete Field Guide

H.B. Lock

--

Get a job.

—

--

--

--

--

--

--

--

--

--

--

--

--

--

--

--

--

--

--

--

--

--

--

--

--

--

--

--

--

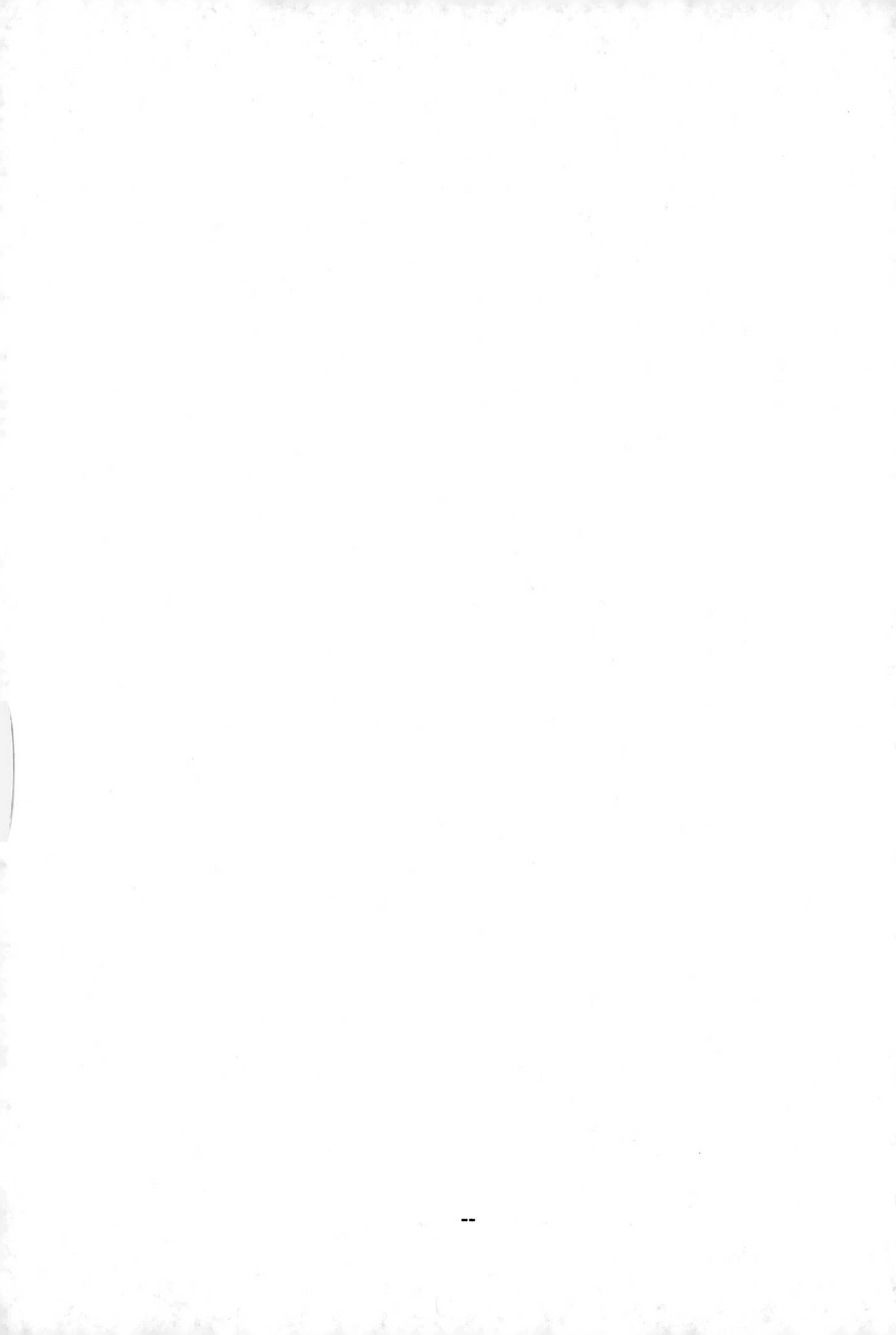

--

--

www.ingramcontent.com/pod-product-compliance
Lightning Source LLC
Chambersburg PA
CBHW061341250726
48657CB00004B/1266